GW01375525

Contents

Jake

Go to Sleep, Bear

Molly's Dreams

Big Fat Cat

Tell Me a Story

Bedtime Stories for the Very Young

Stories by Mathew Price
Illustrations by Atsuko Morozumi

Mathew Price Limited

Text copyright © 2003 Mathew Price
Illustrations copyright © 2003 Atsuko Morozumi
Designed by Douglas Martin
All rights reserved

ISBN 1-84248-158-4
This edition first published 2005 by Mathew Price Limited
The Old Glove Factory, Bristol Road
Sherborne, Dorset DT9 4HP
Manufactured in China

Jake

Jake's Mummy had a new baby.
All day long she was rocking it and cuddling it.

She had no time for Jake.

Jake decided he would run away.
He took his teddy and set off into the woods.

In the woods he met a bear.
'I'm going to eat you up' said the bear.

'Don't be silly' said Jake.
'You can give me a ride if you like'.

Round a bend in the path, they met a wolf.
'I'm going to eat you up,' said the wolf.

'No, you're not,' said Jake. 'Move over.'
The wolf was surprised. He felt a little faint and went off to lie down.

A little further on they met a tiger.
'I'm going to eat you up,' said the tiger.

'No you're not,' said Jake. 'Shouldn't you be in a zoo?'
'Oh,' said the tiger. 'Perhaps. I'll think about it.'

By this time Jake was hungry. 'That's enough running away for today,' he said. 'You can take me home now.'

When he got home his Mummy hugged him tight. 'Why did you run away?' she asked. 'You don't love me any more,' said Jake.

'Of course I love you,' said his Mummy.
'Come on, snuggle up.'

THE END

Go to Sleep, Bear

It was bedtime.

Bear and his friends were settling down for the night.
'Goodnight, Mouse. Goodnight, Cat.'
'Goodnight, Bear, sleep well.'

But Bear tossed . . .   and turned . . .   and he couldn't get to sleep.

Suddenly he sat up. 'Oh no!' he said.

'I've forgotten to check the doors and windows.'

The friends settled down again.

'Oh no!' said Bear.

'I forgot to pack my lunch for tomorrow.'

'Go to sleep. Bear.' said Mouse.

And Bear tried to go to sleep.

'Oh no!' said Bear. 'I need to pee.'

'Go to *sleep*, Bear!' said Mouse.

'Go to *sleep*, Bear!' said Cat.

But it was no good . . . there was something he had forgotten . . . 'Oh no!"

'Now what?'

'I forgot to give you a goodnight kiss.'

They all settled down to sleep.

'Goodnight, Bear,' said Mouse . . .

'Goodnight, Bear,' said Cat . . .

But Bear was fast asleep.

THE END

Molly's Dreams

These dream pictures have lots going on in them, so that you can make up your own stories about all that is happening.

Jungle

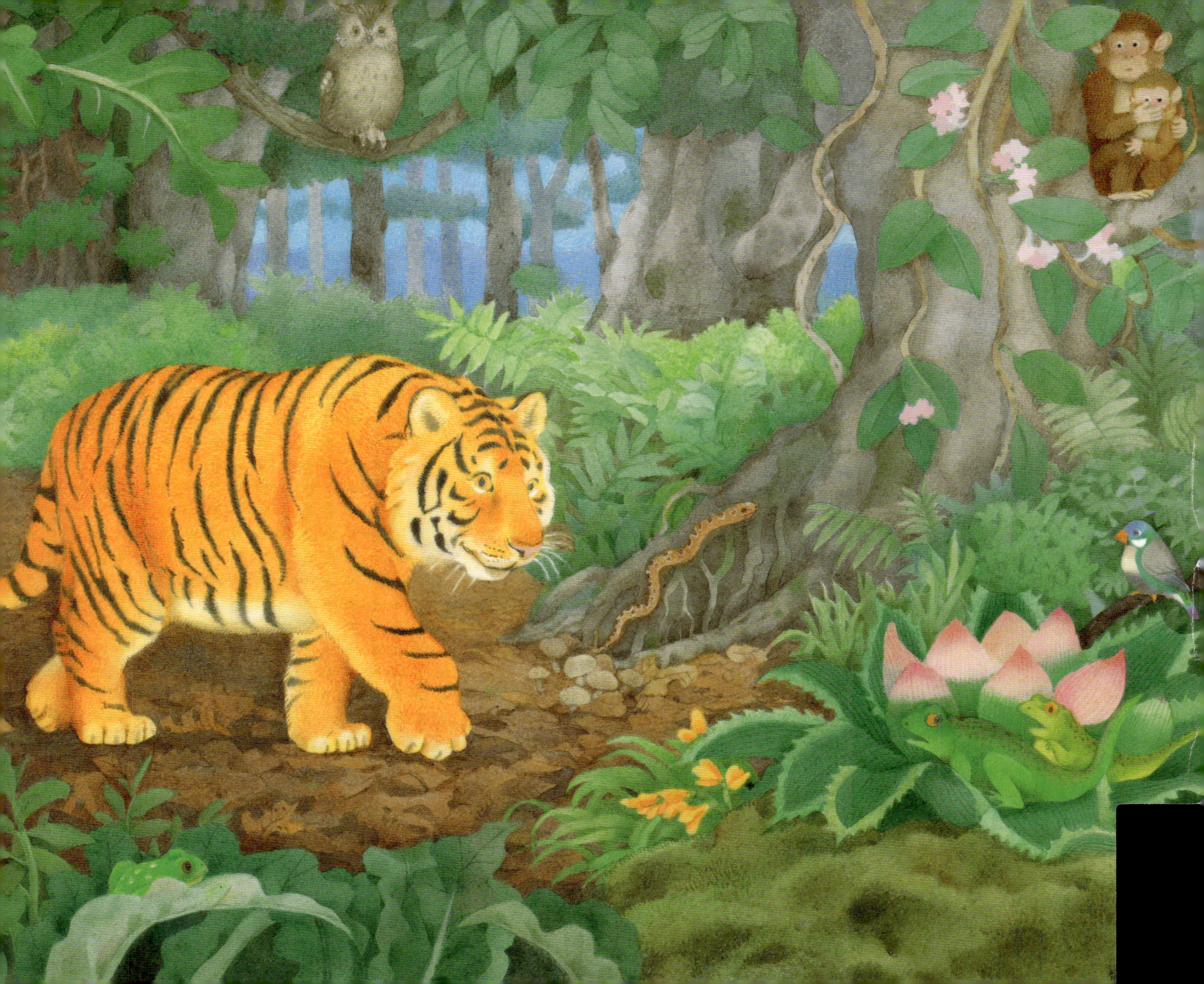

Teddy's House

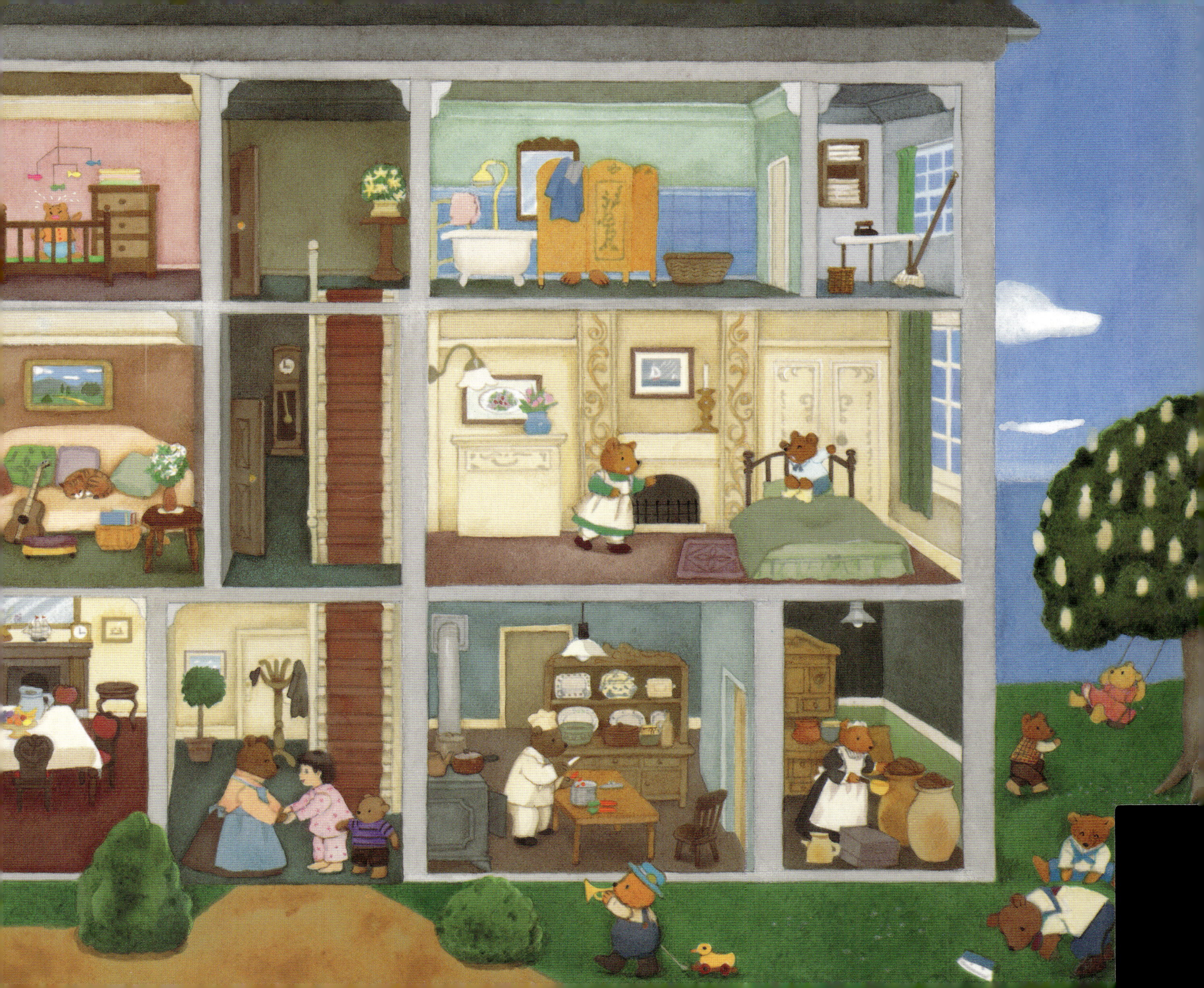

Under the Sea

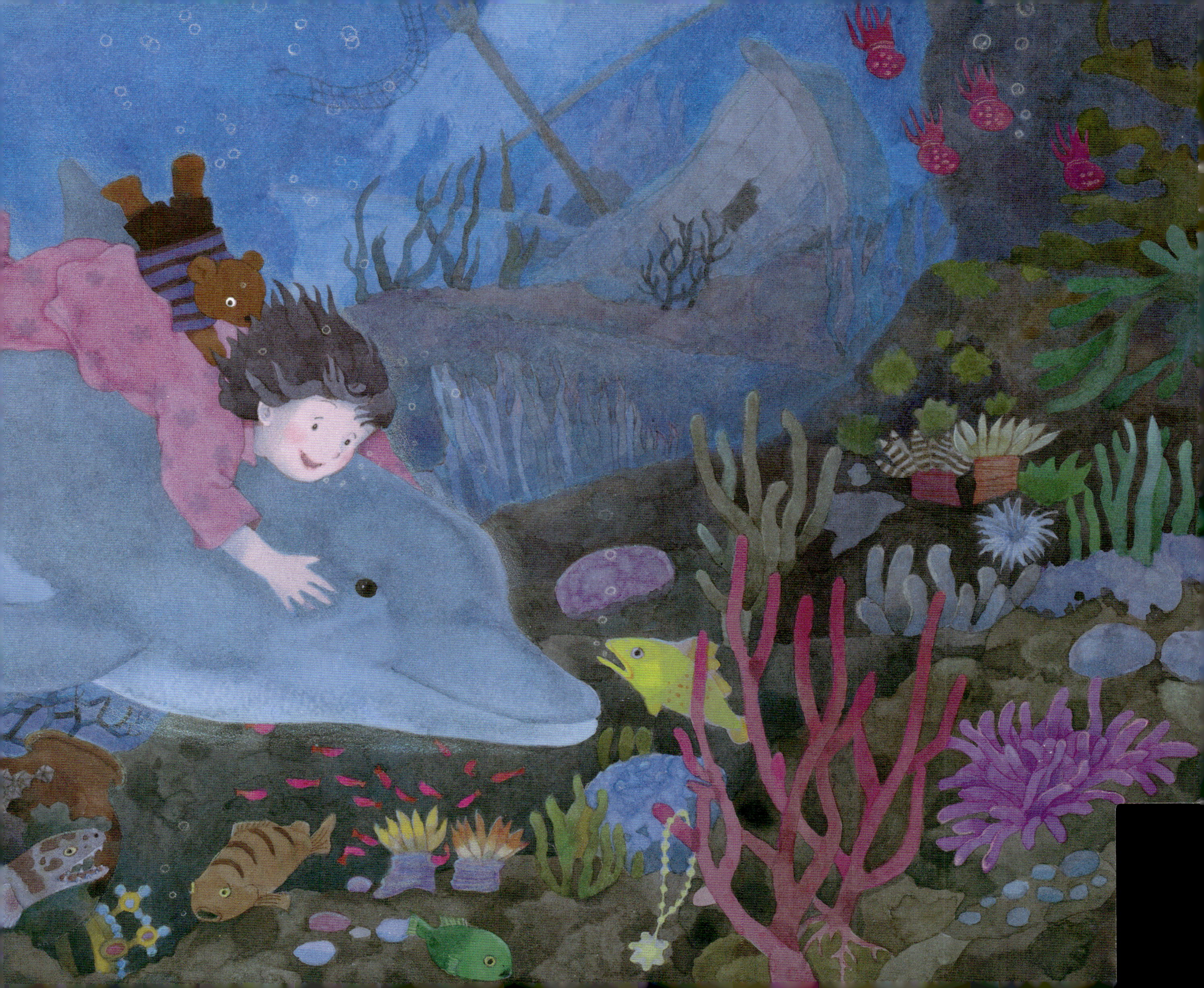

Dinosaurs

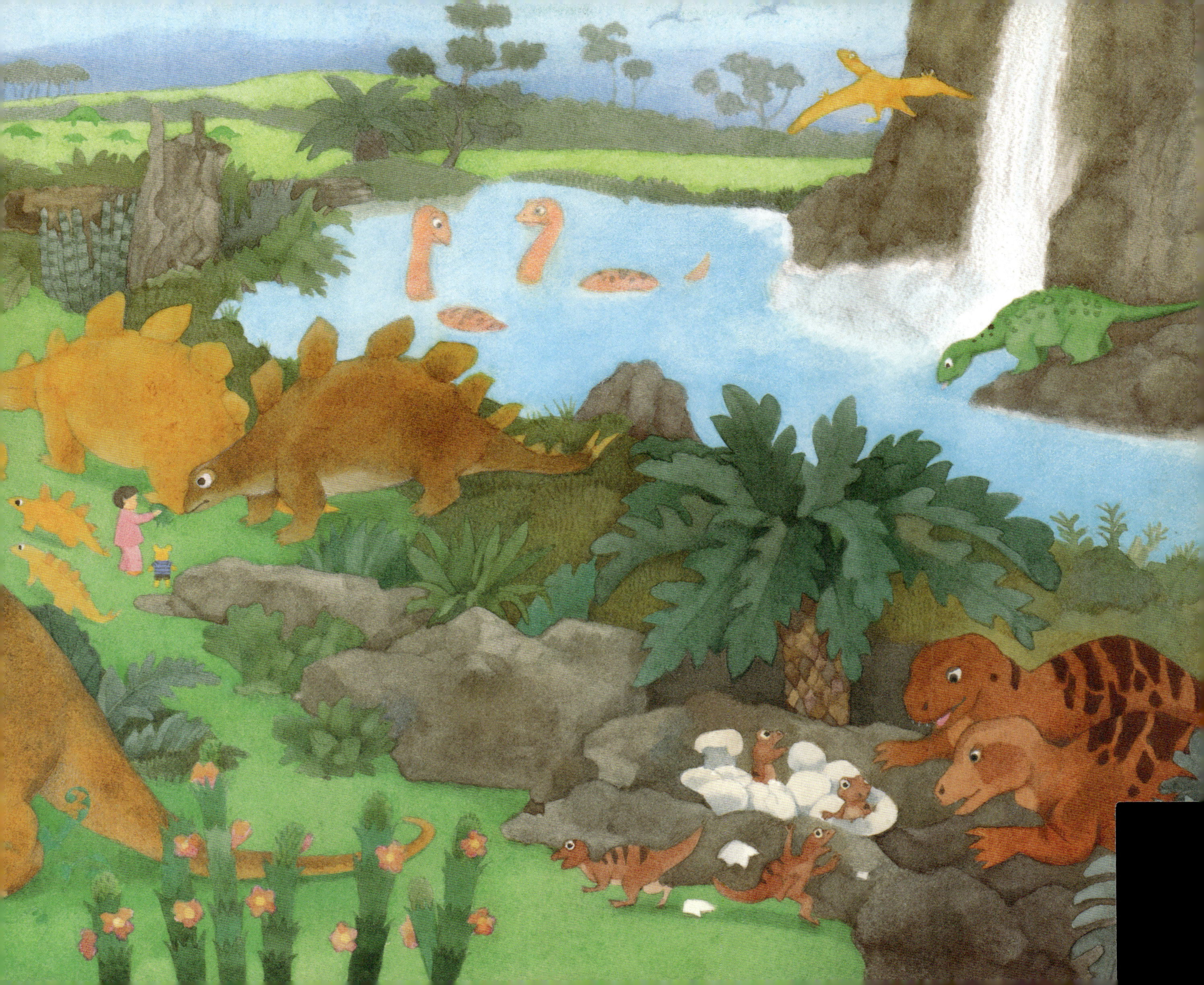

THE END

Big Fat Cat

It was time for supper and the Big Fat Cat was hungry. So he went to look for some milk.

First he met a duck.

'Dear duck', said the Big Fat Cat. 'Can I have some milk?'
'Ducks don't have milk', said the duck. 'Ask someone else'.

'Of course', said the Big Fat Cat.
'I knew that'.
And he went to ask the tortoise.

'Dear Tortoise,' said
the Big Fat Cat.
'Can I have some milk?'

'Tortoises don't
have milk', said
the tortoise.

'Of course', said the Big Fat Cat.
'I knew that'.
And he went to see porcupine.

'Dear Porcupine,' said the Big Fat Cat, 'Can I have some milk?'
'Some milk?' said the porcupine. 'Porcupines don't have milk. Ask someone else'.

'Of course', said the Big Fat Cat. 'I knew that'.
So he went to see the hippo.

'Dear Hippo,' said the Big Fat Cat,
'Can I have some milk?'

'Some milk?'
 said the hippo,
'Some milk?'

And he laughed and laughed and laughed.

'Don't you know anything?' he said.
'You don't get milk from a hippo,
you get milk from a cow.'

'Of course', said the Big Fat Cat.
'I knew that'.
And he went to look for the cow.

'Dear Cow,' said the Big Fat Cat,
'Can *you* give me some milk?'
'Of course,' said the cow.
'Help yourself.'

Then the Big Fat Cat was very happy. He had three large bowls of milk . . .

. . . and fell fast asleep.

THE END

Tell Me a Story

James had put on his pyjamas . . . cleaned his teeth . . .

picked up his teddy
from the bottom of the stairs . . . and climbed onto his Mummy's lap.

'Tell me a story,' he said.
'A story?' said his Mummy. 'Well let me see.'

Once there was a little mouse who lived in the roots of an old oak tree.

He was trying to sleep but it was very cold.

So he got some straw and some leaves and some feathers,

and made himself a nest.

It was so warm and cosy that very soon he was fast asleep.

Once there was a lion who lived in the jungle.
He was trying to sleep but it was too noisy.

So he gave a huge

Roar!

For a moment all was quiet and the lion settled down in his den.
Soon all the noises began again, but the lion was fast asleep.

Once there was a tortoise who lived in the desert.
He was trying to sleep but it was too hot.

So he started to dig a hole.

And he dug . . .

and he dug . . .

and he dug.

And he made himself a little bedroom under the ground.

It was cool and safe and very soon he fell asleep.

Once there was an owl.
In the morning when
everybody was getting up
she was ready to go to
sleep.

So she flew into
the darkest part of
the tree . . .

. . . and settled
down on a branch.

She looked so like the tree that nobody knew she was there, and soon she was fast asleep.

'And once,' said James's Mummy, 'There was a little boy . . .'

But that little boy was fast asleep. So she picked him up carefully . . .

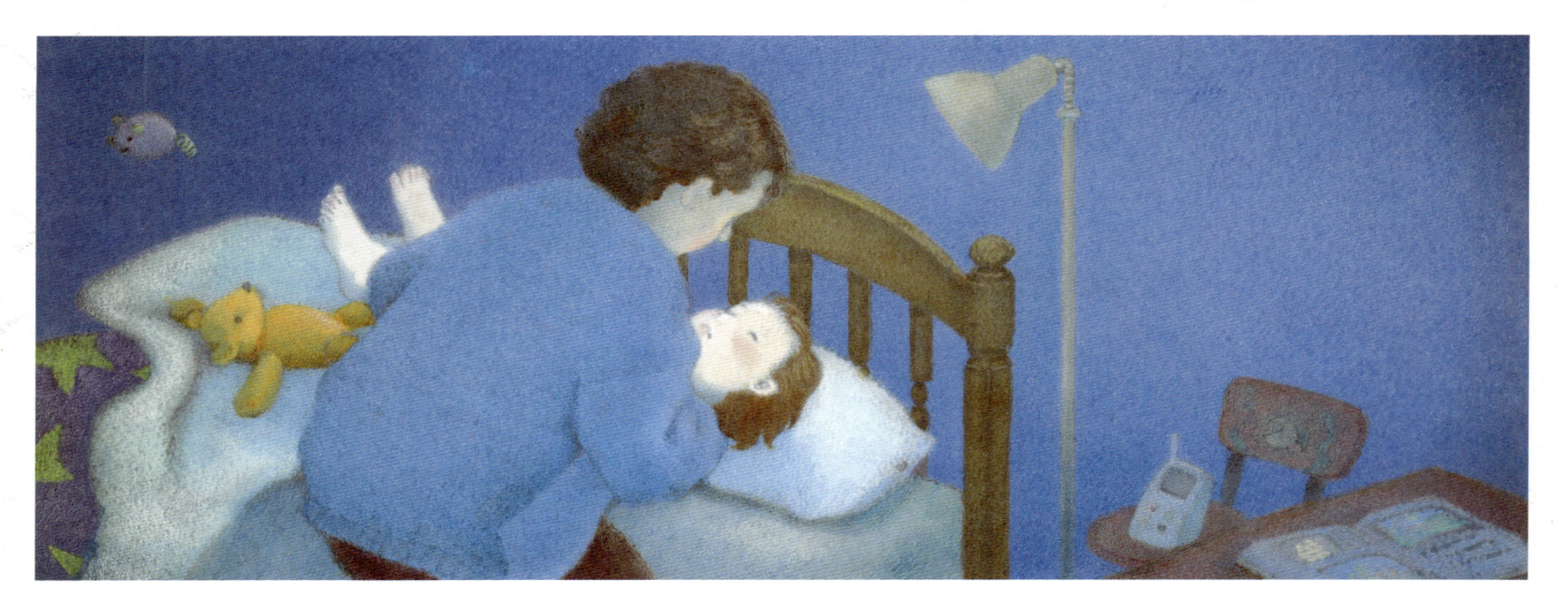

. . . and put him in his bed.

. . . 'Good night, sweet heart,' she said, 'sweet dreams.'

THE END